Butterflies

in my

Stomach

CHRIS ELESE

CHRIS ELESE

Butterflies in My Stomach
ISBN: 978-1-7346285-6-2

One2Mpower Publishing LLC. one2mpower@gmail.com
www.one2mpower.com Ordering Information: Quantity sales:
Printed in the United States of America

"A young black woman choosing transparency for the healing of herself and for others."

First, I would like to say thanks and glory to GOD for allowing me to embrace my truth and enable me to share my testimony the best way I know how. Secondly, I hope this book serves as an example to my daughter, that anything is possible once you commit to achieving it.

Please allow this collection of art to serve you in whatever capacity you naturally feel moved. My earnest thoughts simply spilled out on paper in the form of poems, prose, quotes, affirmations, and monologues.

Currently, at the age of 27, I have learned if I don't love myself then no one else will. If I can't laugh at myself then everyone else will. I choose to stop beating myself up for not completing everything, the way in which I want it. To stop standing in my own way! Instead, I choose to love and care for myself more than ever. I deserve the world! Done trying to figure out God's plan for my life, because when he places me in a room, He has already given me the credentials to be there. So, I choose to thrive there and do so while loving myself!

In the years that I have known the author, joy has been the dominant emotion I have experienced from our relationship. Joy is defined as "the emotion of great delight or happiness caused by something exceptionally good or satisfying; keen pleasure; elation." And although we wish we could shield our loved ones from anything that would try to steal their joy, we can't. We can only hope they can see the light ahead and make it through any darkness with minimal bruising or harm. *Butterflies in my Stomach* creatively reflects many circumstances and relationships—some that haven't always been joyful for Elese. But it also lets me know that she has always had within what she needs to take her through to the place where joy awaits her.

- Evelyn Carter

CHRIS ELESE

butterflies in my stomach

suppressed feelings
now developed
into full grown thoughts
anxiously waiting to be said
to be heard
to be valued

- My Butterfly Release

CHRIS ELESE

I   CATERPILLAR
II   A'RBOL
III   MY RYE
IV   ROYAL PURPLE
V   RAINBOW
VI   SEVEN

I   CATERPILLAR

always good enough to be the best friend,
but not the wife.

why apply all this effort in the beginning
if you're just going to quit
in the middle?

CHRIS ELESE

to hear the news
over the phone
from overseas
that my husband committed adultery
that's a new level of
intimacy

Butterflies in My Stomach

I don't know
I don't know what to do next
how to get over you
how to "cope" with life here
now with no you
no clear clarity or closure
just no you
no more kisses on my forehead or
"good morning" text
just no you
no more vocabulary trivia late night
just no you
no more giving me the run down on your family
just no you
no more opening the door for me
just no you
no more of your insightful business plans
just no you
no more you inquiring about my perspective
just no you
no more creative vibes in the studio
just no you
no more of dreaming your heart out with me
just no you
no more you

CHRIS ELESE

two weeks after the divorce was final
his second child was born.

you ignored me
locked my voice up
for far too long

CHRIS ELESE

I refuse to cry a river for you
care enough to change my mood for you
change my decisions
my life
alter me
for you
you deserve a prayer and
a "see you later"
a later that never crosses paths again
after your choice to lie
choice to lay down with her
choice to walk away
from your family
your "best" friend
your til death do you part
yet you haven't died
it's a shame really
that you waste time
uttering words from your mouth
that will change
as quick as the clock strikes midnight
time is up

remember
these cold nights, wishing they were warm ones
those cozy arms, wishing they were wrapped tight
around my mind
because I'm willing to sacrifice the physical
if it means having it all in the end
having without the slightest form of doubt
that you will continue to walk back into our home
everyday
because you choose to be there
choose to commit
choose to love
choose to embrace
to never lighten your grip
your grasp of
what you prayed for
worked for
damn near knocked down my walls for

CHRIS ELESE

even after it all
I wake up to our child
vomiting on me at 3am

when does the driving force behind the chase end?

    a.   when you obtain what you sought out for
    b.   when you are no longer fulfilled
    c.   when you fail to push yourself over the
        hump/ quit yourself

        survey says:

    d.   when you fail to push yourself over the
        hump/ quit yourself -97%

waking up with you inside of me
was an icky feeling
one of distress and heartache
so, I chose the only action my body had energy to
make
inactivity
I laid there
took it...
like many do
but can't fathom to pierce their lips to say
I don't know if I was more upset in your act
or that you didn't think asking me was even an
option anymore
or that you no longer had a regard for me
then I should have known our marriage was broken
with no room to repair
thinking that our commitment to each other
solidified a way in at all times
when I am dead sleep
then wake up to this
penetrating more than my walls
my heart was shattered
then I knew you were capable of befriending the
same type of person
it all clicked
that college night

when you chose not to hold him accountable for
doing the same to my sister
I should have known before this moment
you knew
you knew and brushed it off
like a bad fart in the wind
never to be spoken of
but the ill smell lingered
all these thoughts
while I laid there

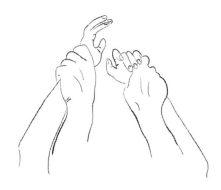

CHRIS ELESE

I fell in love with the you I met.
I ran away from the you I came to know.

initially in a cocoon
trapped
forced to grow
to grow up
before I was ready

wrapped into this new unbearable lifestyle
that's nothing like the housewives we see on tv
more so the unpleasant
catering to others
at their beck and call
they called me mom
and wife
not artist
not author
not me
not who I wanted to be
yet I kept filling their cups to half full
while mine
well my pitcher was half empty

you loved
crown royal
like you were a king
but in actuality
you were far from it

once you give him your heart
it's supposed to be no breaking apart
those three little words "I love you"
you thought he meant them too
but being in the real world nothing last forever
were just not meant to be together
you hurt me a hell of a lot, but I forgave you and
tried to refill your spot
but all the others didn't cut it... but you
you were my addiction
my heart, my mind, and soul my whole body
exhibition
this feeling that I had it's over now and I'm glad
glad I know now I deserve so much more then you
no more depression because my happiness is past
due
living for myself not letting you determine how I
feel
because now I know what's real
now after everything you want me back
but it's cute how your mind thinks like that
that despite the past we can still be
but my reply was no, I can't believe I said that me
I'm stronger than I think I am

I choose you
..... not the reflection that I see in the mirror every
day or the voice that echoes through my ears
but you, the real you
the positive one, the one that appreciates what she
has because to her the little things mean everything
when you're happy
I want the one who doesn't care about what others
may think, say, or do to her because she knows who
really matters
the one person she tries to impress
her love
her life
her everything
herself
I choose the one who made me fall in love with
myself

CHRIS ELESE

I took on his life
like it was mine
like I couldn't function
with just my own
like my own was nothing without his
worth nothing
by hiding from my own
I hindered myself from
my family's love
my love for the arts
my own values and standard of living
my political opinions
my creative thoughts and ideas
me
I ran away from myself by
running into him
compromising on every turn
until there was no more of me left
no more of me to show
like the first seventeen years without him
were magically erased
gone
vanished
just like that

all because I chose to take on his life as my own

CHRIS ELESE

how do I even begin to
explain to another the
dirt you left me in

CHRIS ELESE

after two years of abandonment
I finally had to see you face to face
in the court room
my nerves getting the best of me
us fighting over the frivolous notions
our lawyers brought up
until finally my lawyer told me
loose the battle
win the war
so, I had to say I did something minuscule wrong
in order for the judge to see
all your larger wrongdoings
to me
to my baby
at that moment the ruling
turned in my favor

I should have been thrilled
but who wants to sit and hear
you
the you I once loved
for a large portion of your life
say
that our relationship
is broken beyond repair
how quickly you answered,
"yes, your honor"

is how fast my heart sank

I looked down
then up again
faking the last bit of strength
I had left
to sign my
divorce papers with a
smile

CHRIS ELESE

II   A'RBOL

Butterflies in My Stomach

hear the birds chirping
light beaming through the glass
crust falling from your eyes
yawn spoiling from your mouth's breath
it's an awakening
another opportunity
another adventure worth taking
another story worth telling
another fight worth learning from
another choice to be made
another welcoming of change
it's…
it's morning
what some dread
while others pray for it
take it
as is
use it
do what your heart desire with it
but don't not experience it

CHRIS ELESE

slow to anger,
but quick to understanding.

when is the last time you generously gave?
like you expect others to give to you.

CHRIS ELESE

erroneous intent
is more hindering
than inadequate action

invest in you
the inner you
not your appearance
not by getting monthly
wax appointments
nails/toe appointments
hair appointment
eyebrow appointments
all that money
and time spent on your appearance
you cheated yourself out of
a more meaningful investment
more meaningful you
think about it

unlearning is hard. we're only taught how to learn.
be patient with this new process.

how to avoid growing pains:
-    settle
-    be complacent
-    never love yourself
-    numb yourself
-    die

stimulate my mind,
and my body will do the rest.

Butterflies in My Stomach

balance on my toes
balance my thoughts
my intake
my love
balance everything
they say too much of anything
isn't good for you…
so balance
like it's as easy as walking a straight line on your
girls night out
as easy as parting your natural hair in a straight line
on the first try
as easy as muting your thoughts and just being
as easy as loving the right person
perfectly
but don't quit
continue to balance
or succeed at trying
because it's all a balancing act

sometimes in real life you not only have to go back
a few steps,
but also go back to start.

ignoring a red flag
will eliminate your chances of experiencing a green
one

CHRIS ELESE

twenty-six
divorced
with a four-year-old
priorities adjust

thankful for
my master's degree
a decent paying job
the apartment
the means to feed, clothe, & spoil
my child
the village we created around us
of family, and friends
without God
providing them, there would be no
forward moment

no becoming a first-time homeowner
no great education for my baby
no scholarship providing extracurriculars for her
no having a career and my own business
no new chance of a love that I never fathomed to
experience before

nothing more

Butterflies in My Stomach

unlearn that my voice and desires don't matter.

unlearn that I can depend on anyone else but God for anything.

unlearn beating myself up over past mistakes, actions, and choices.

unlearn settling and accepting what is only presented to me, instead of patiently waiting for what is deserving of me.

unlearn that because many African Americans are financially illiterate, it's alright for me to be content with making ends meet and having one source of income.

unlearn to not post pictures of myself, and instead love on me regardless if they don't compare to these Instagram models.

unlearn that it is better to live comfortably in hell instead of taking the challenging journey to live in peace.

plant seeds and watch how they
alter your environment.

CHRIS ELESE

vulnerability is at the core of us
the beauty of who we are
the raw, uncut, canvas of us
we so naturally hide or stray from us
the essence of our being
because we learned to filter life as if it's the real
fantasy
as if pimples or dark spots are a faded pigment of
our imagination

men are the number one predators for women
the cause for losses and insecurities
death and births
just to experience more deaths
imprisoned in the idea of "love"
that it can move mountains
erase abuse
& make you believe that all the bullshit is worth
enduring
that comes with choosing to ride for him
the reason why we as women hate on each other
just to be perceived as ahead in "his" eyes
when we end up in the same place
of being displaced by men

moving blind is both a blessing and a curse
it's choosing to allow the environment to lead you
mold you
teach you
transform you into what you believe is pure
intentional bliss
until you get cut
yet you shockingly have that dumbfounded look on
your face
as to why it hurts
more importantly
why did you agree to be blindfolded?

functional depression is real
feeding your kid
waiting for them to go to sleep
just to finally feel like you can take your own life
but you still don't
you wake up the next morning
steady taking care of their hierarchy of needs
just going through the motions
until the next time life throws you curve balls and
you don't know how to breathe
don't know how to function in your depression
don't know how to function in your life anymore
until it's not as easy to sweep your mess up under a
rug
and function

CHRIS ELESE

what gives you peace?
get it and hold on to it.

Butterflies in My Stomach

goals:

-wear lipstick every day!
-write a book of prose & poetry
-own my own land
-love on myself daily
-get out my own way
-dance/ exercise as often as possible
-treat others better than they treat me
-save and tithe/ offering money back to God on a
consistent basis – he is the best investment!
-stay true to myself always

XOXO Chris Elese

CHRIS ELESE

III   MY RYE

.

Invest in you.

do it for the love and nothing else
for GOD is love
and love never fails.

art is my first love.
it has saved me time and time again.

that moment when you stop
allowing life to happen to you
and choose to move intentionally.

traded in a wedding ring, baby bottle, & an apron
for peace of mind, a pair of pointe shoes, & a bible.

CHRIS ELESE

I can't explain the feeling
the pure joy
you taught me
through my own body

I am in the position
where I need art to rescue me again
I choose to no longer allow
life to happen to me and live by
reactions based on others
uncontrollable actions
I choose to live intentionally
I choose to live for myself

how to turn pain
into a painting
sorrow into
a song
distress into
a hit drama
life gives you
all the reason
to create

to see the light
in my daughters
smile
allows me to
see the world
differently

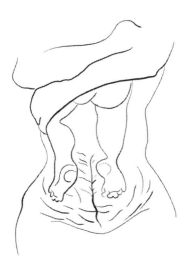

writing for you.

I choose to see the
delight in your eyes
especially when you
refuse to see it for yourself

beautiful full lips
Chinese slanted eyes
small waist with them thick thighs
the perfect shade of caramel
small belly to match
perfect size boobs for any mouth to catch
dark natural curly hair
but she still wears weave
waiting around for another nigga to appease

couldn't you hear this on the radio?
I bet if some rapper were to say these words
in such a smooth way
to the catchiest of beats
these words would be memorized immediately
why does society celebrate such
art?

if you're too embarrassed to ask for help
you're too afraid to grow.

you teach me
something new
you teach me
how to deal with myself
face myself
treat myself
appreciate myself

how can I be so afraid
of something
I once loved?

natural is a mindset,
a lifestyle,
a freedom.
stop living by society's rules,
and begin to create your own!

the laughter behind
those jokes
the vivid picture
 coming through
those brush strokes
keep me coming for more

the worst thing you can do to me
is take away my appreciation of the arts.

when all else fails
throw on some
lipstick & heels
-confident essentials

when I write
it's powerful
I am powerful
when I write I am who I aspire to be
why can't this confident,
unapologetic, proud, strong,
resilient women show up
in person
in the boardroom
in the church
in the community
in the household
in love with someone
that truly has the
capacity to nurture
yet build me up and still
restrain me
from all the world has to offer
that will dim my light

you are my
reason why

CHRIS ELESE

alpha project:
-start, regardless of what that looks like
-alter your approach if needed
-embrace the unknown
-react to defeat as a win, celebrate & continue again
-give it your all (I promise you won't regret it)
-passion/faith the size of a mustard seed

XOXO Chris Elese

IV   ROYAL PURPLE

it hurts to feel it
to deal with it
to accept it
rather just ignore
not process the rejection
it's too much to handle
I'll crack
break down to a place
so foreign
I don't know that I will
ever come back from it
a scary feeling
what Lil Wayne refers
to as the halo in
the trash
because I can't
fathom to reflect
on the past
the what about me feeling
the ignored
muffled feeling
the I'm suffocating
from the overpowering
sounds of
nothing
because nobody is there

don't trust someone too
close to the edge

CHRIS ELESE

I want to always be honest with you
about me
my past
my struggles
my wrongdoings
but
how can I do that
and
still inspire you
guide you in the right directions
since my actions only reflect how lost I am

tick tick
tok
can't get that second back.

for as long as I can remember I've had this fight
a strong passionate fight that urged to seep out
at the very sight or thought of disagreement
this was my form of protection
that I sought out to give myself
instead this safety mechanism turned out to be the
very thing that I needed protection from
see I never understood the extent and the source in
which my pain derived
it was easier and clearer to blame the one who was
on the opposing side of me
instead of reflecting on the far from sturdy ground I
stood on
the ground I would swear by
I would take my last breath for
that's how strongly I believed in me
in my beliefs, opinions, and experiences
myself
who knew the stance I would die for was the real
issue
deep down I was aware all along, but I chose to
overlook it
a choice that almost cost me myself
I chose not to believe that the one I needed
protection from the most was me

Butterflies in My Stomach

I used to believe with all my heart my unwavering
passion and determination was my strength, but in
actuality it has been a slow death sentence
holding me back
deteriorating me

love me…
all I wanted was for you to love me
since love is the "greatest"
it should eventually come and find me
find me through the pain
the scars
the nightmares that turn out to be reality
the unfulfilled expectations
the journey
trenches of mistakes, losses, and false hope
keep me grounded, sane, above water
keep me coming back for me
every time
over again
keep me to reciprocate forgiveness
even when I don't earn it
constantly fighting for that comeback
that come up
the rise of my jaw
on both side of my cheeks
then and only then did I realize
that loving me is an inside job
and the only fulfillment to take heed of
is my own love
self-love
my planted, created, and fostered love
therefore, no more "love me"

naw, I love me

CHRIS ELESE

the greatest pressure
are those beady little eyes
that watch my every move

can I ignore the pregnancy
the growth of innocence
when the ironic truth
is the creation of such a beauty
is oh so ugly
so disgusting
so hurtful…
you came from two lost people
who made a bad choice
a choice collectively to put their
physical desires before your sisters
emotional health
people who gave no regard for a marriage
a home
a family
people whose only concern was for themselves
and not for the many lives they were affecting
how a married father of one would walk away so
easily
then create you
I don't blame you
I can't blame you
crazy thing is I love you
you don't even know it
hopefully one day you will
but for my health
and your sister's

CHRIS ELESE

I have to isolate us
from you
from them
from your life

Butterflies in My Stomach

I can't please you
if it's not one thing
then it's another
every action
every decision
every word
you overbear
can't live that way
shit that's no way to live

sometimes I don't feel
good enough for you

is "love" worth it?
worth the risk worth the pain
worth the unknown
worth going years and waking up to a complete
stranger
worth losing yourself
worth dying for
is "love" worth it?

CHRIS ELESE

some decisions
lead to more decisions
but do what's best for you
they will become easier to make

Butterflies in My Stomach

I'm tired of it
I'm tired of hurting
tired of worrying about money
tired of living like this
tired of living in this unhealthy
cycle of the same shitty mess
I choose not to live in the
same place
the place where you left me
the dirt you left me in
I am now
choosing better
choosing more for me
without you
without everything that
made me sad and tired
I am choosing no longer
to live without myself

-tragedy of losing oneself

CHRIS ELESE

too numb to
remember

when the conversations
grow beyond the surface?
when you are your unfiltered self
unapologetically?
when you all's words grow into
a healthy debate until
the other respectfully declares
the genius of the other's thought process
or when you articulate your
flaws, worries, weaknesses,
or shit you're just not proud of?
even then how do you know their intentions
unless you ask, even though that's as basic of a
topic to ensue and you don't want to ruin the flow
of the conversation with such a minuscule idea
will you even really know then though?
know that you could have fascinating
communication about everything else but you two
will you never without a doubt know that as close
are you are you can't always have those simple yet
perplexed conversations that ultimately need to be
discussed

-trust issues/courageous conversations

CHRIS ELESE

I know I love him
we vibed from those
innocent freshmen year of college talks
til now
eight years later
now
a kid by someone else
later
now
sex with his roommate
later
now
a broken heart
later
now
a deep depression
later
now
we still talk
still love
still vibe
to the tone of each other's voices
still support
each other
still appreciate
each other
that's why I know

Butterflies in My Stomach

I know I love him (*Gucci mane voice*)

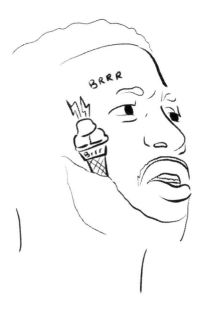

constant thoughts
deprive your
current experiences

mature enough to know that
I am only responsible for my own actions
own intentions, motives, & words
can't keep beating myself up over you
the situation
poor timing, choices, communication
back then I didn't have it all together
I swear going with the flow and playing off your
moves was my only move
instead of speaking up for you, when you were
voiceless
defending you, when you weren't aware you needed
protection
assisting you to find the words that came to your
heart, but never upon your lips
showing you that I loved you regardless
that my immaturity was all to get your attention
to have you notice me
I know now that
in the midst of your rape
your heartache
your pain
I stood there
not knowing how to help you
not being what you needed me to be

with facts, still comes perception.

the heart is more deceiving
than we give it credit for.

CHRIS ELESE

V   RAINBOW

Butterflies in My Stomach

it's alright to choose you first
even though that may look like you
not owing someone an explanation
not continuing a relationship of twenty plus years
not indulging in your first true love
letting go of what no longer serves you
is just as powerful, brave, & constructive as what
used to make you happy
you now take your control back
your time back
your values back
you back
regardless if you appear selfish, or stubborn
you chose you
for once
they will learn to get used to it
or you will learn that it's the only choice worth
choosing

status quo:
-get married
-have a baby
-happy ever after

reality:
-get pregnant
-discover self-love
-live not just survive

be the soil for your grass
be the sunlight for your herbs
be the water for your flowers
be the oxygen for your garden.

surround yourself
with those who will not hesitate
to place a mirror in your face.

when God is in your life, there is no need to play the victim.

create & do so while loving yourself!

Butterflies in My Stomach

self-love is important
it gives you the ability to receive grace
then being big enough to be receptive of it
positive words and thoughts
allow you to hold yourself through the
bullshit the world brings
pick yourself up through the storm
hold your head up high
always

CHRIS ELESE

phrase:
sparkling our crowns

definition:
– the feeling you get when your hair is freshly done

today you have the opportunity
to rewrite your story.
go ahead
just pick up
the pen.

it's healthy to dream
healthy to take your mind to elsewhere
beyond your physical situation

oh, what is that
hiding behind that pain
is that hope
is that courage
is that the love
willing
to try again?

thank you lord,
for I know your plan is just beginning.

pray for your enemies
no matter how hard it hurts.

take that leap baby
promise it will be worth the fall
don't look down
keep your eyes on me
don't let go
I got you

be impulsive for a reason.
step out on faith & don't
look back, because if
certain people are not moving with you
then they weren't meant to understand.

CHRIS ELESE

we are
results of our grandmother's prayers

the first step into
expecting others to accept your flaws
is for you to love them.

faith in God is what you need
in order to survive
it's a breaking point when you no longer choose to
utilize your words to vent your experiences and
emotions
instead you choose life through God
when you decide whole heartedly to take the
worldly beating and turn the other cheek, because
you know he will never leave you or forsake you
it's the air that allows you to breathe into the next
day
the nudge you receive to get up even when the
weight holding you down seems unbearable to
surpass
the silent yet admirable rainbow after the
tumultuous storm
the tool to elevate you to a peace that withdraws
you from simple-minded people and things
it allows you to unapologetically appreciate taking a
deep breath
and breathe
breathe through the naysayers
breathe through the heartache
breathe through worldly opinions
(that seem to fluctuate as often as the wind blows)
breathe through the tears
then move by faith

move with an intentional effort, knowing that
regardless of what it looks like
it's already yours

why value and continue to
pour your soul
into those who
don't even care
to see
how you are doing

his inability to see my beauty
enabled me to see my own.

CHRIS ELESE

VI   SEVEN

it's never fun to be right.

that may have been his best, sis
shame on you for asking for more than what he is
currently capable of.

true integrity starts with
not lying to yourself.

accept people for where they are
who they are
because that is probably
all they are able to give you.

what is so enchanting about me is
I am the strongest force that can stop me
the same amount of effort and love that I give
myself can't be matched
see the sweet nothings, kind gestures, and money
spent
can't compete
with my daily affirmations, restful meditations, and
all the self-love I choose to give
see that's the problem though
all the love, support, and encouragement I have
been longing for
the dynamic life changing, dramatically movie
fantasized ending
resides in what I give myself
I was mad angry, at all the yous, hims, and thems
when in actuality I was mad at me
me
for not giving me what I was seeking externally
with the time and energy I took on hating
everything and everybody else
I could have just been reflecting on me
healing from me
finally, appreciative for turning the mirror around
for allowing my comprehension to see that the sole
reason for my frown

was me
is me
will always be me.

.

October 26th, 2018 is when you finally said it out loud. your actions and even inactions have always showed me, but that day you said it. the words came out of your mouth. it's no way you can ever take them back. you told me, it is hard for you to love me. it is challenging for you to deal with me, ever since I was born. therefore, you choose not to emotionally support me. you chose to isolate me. your "I love yous" were merely statements with nothing meaningful behind them. how could the person I spent nine months growing in be so detached from me. as fiercely as the pain of hearing nails scrape a chalkboard, that's how displaced I felt. you continued on and elaborated by claiming loving my brother and my own child was easier for you, than to love me. those are the words that came out of your mouth. I don't believe your words hurt me, due to our many lifeless interactions over the years. what pierced the most was that you had no reason to refrain from saying it any longer.

stop giving people
more of you
than they deserve.

the moment you decide to worry
is the same moment you quit on yourself.

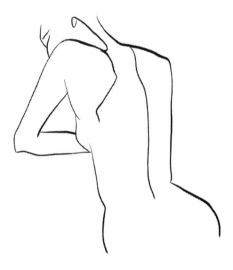

unfortunately, too often
we choose convenience over commitment.

as a woman I am already
silenced
put in my place
ignored
too emotional to hold a position of power
similar severity to a scarlet letter on my back

as an African American
I can be killed for the
skin I am in
with no
legislative reprimand
for my demise

see, as a black woman
I am supposed to lift up my black brothers
polish their crowns, and be their backbone
as needed
I am supposed to advocate for other women
vocalize prochoice initiatives, and vote for the
women candidates
if they make the ballot

see as a black woman
who is there for me?
I bare a unique
burden on my back

and they wonder why
I am angry…

too valuable to entertain
anything less than love.

choose your battles

hair
vs
more meaningful things to do with your time.

where your focus is there your heart will be also.
where your time is there your mind will be also.

CHRIS ELESE

lord please
forgive me

who would possibly have ever thought
that one day
the mathematician
the dancer
the dyslexic
one
could express herself with words

CHRIS ELESE

in transition
between the life I aspire to have
and my reality, which is ever-changing
changing from a happy home.

Butterflies in My Stomach

for so long
women of color learned to
express themselves through their hair
resulting in a multi-million dollar industry
that they don't even profit from
their thick rich locs not as easily
imitated by majority of straight thin strands
that premiere on display images
that retail for more
than they are worth

why is that?
ever heard of the doll experiment
the same reason the results
were the Caucasian doll
every time

let's do the experiment again today
59 years later
would the results
be the same?

CHRIS ELESE

why weave
why place the idea of beauty on hair extensions
that can fall out in point three seconds
why waste your time on placing heat to your head
when the moment you get physical your hair
shrivels up
why can't you embrace you
the natural you
the you that rolls out of bed
shakes her pineapple down & seriously can quote
Beyoncé's "I woke up like this"
why can't the coils and curls of your natural hair be
just as beautiful
just as gorgeous to flaunt
just as fierce to give you confidence to conquer the
day
why do you constantly allow other people's opinion
on black hair
determine your daily routine
wear that afro, that twist out, or that wash n' go
wear whatever your true heart's desire is
because the very person you need to please is
you

you are a product of your environment
it influences you whether you choose to give it
weight or not
it teaches your purpose for your chosen actions and
reactions
it molds your likes and dislikes
unconsciously forms your aspirations and desires
guides your determination and most importantly
shapes your lifestyle
your behavior is learned
your life was learned
now it's your choice to unlearn
are you ready?

\

CHRIS ELESE

CHRIS ELESE

healed
heard
honored
now
let's fly

-from me to you

Made in the USA
Columbia, SC
23 July 2020